A PRACTICAL GUIDE
TO
PRODUCTIVITY MEASUREMENT

A PRACTICAL GUIDE
TO
PRODUCTIVITY MEASUREMENT

By Leon Greenberg

*Formerly Executive Director,
National Commission on Productivity*

The Bureau of National Affairs, Inc., Washington, D.C.
1973

Printed in the United States of America
Library of Congress Catalog Card Number: 73-75981
International Standard Book Number: 0-87179-190-0

Type Set in a Union Shop

Table of Contents

v

LIST OF TABLES

CHAPTER 1

Introduction and Concepts

This guide to company productivity measurement is intended to bridge the gap between work measurement and national productivity measurement. It is of interest to those who are concerned with the management of the production of goods and services—including the industrial engineer and the economist as well as the company manager. But it is directed primarily at the latter, to those who assist him in the management of operations, and to his supervisors who may wish to have another measure in addition to the usual operating ratios to evaluate performance of their company.

The productivity measures which can be developed by following the techniques described in this booklet will be compatible with the industry measures developed by government economists. However, the descriptions of concepts and methods will try to avoid the jargon of professional economists in order to provide a "practical" guide to the manager of the factory or other type of enterprise.

What is productivity? It serves no useful purpose to rely on the old cliché that it is whatever the compiler, or reader, or user wishes it to be. Standardization of concepts and a common understanding of what they signify are very important if we are to have a system of information by means of which firms can compare themselves with each other, with the industry and with other industries.

There are some common misunderstandings about productivity. It is not a measure of production although many students of economics and many businessmen have failed to comprehend the difference between productivity and production. It is not a measure of costs, although it is one component of cost. It does not measure

1

the cost of a resource, but it is a measure of the relationship between quantity of resources used and quantity (or value in constant terms) of output. It is not precisely a measure of efficiency, although it is often a good indicator of the efficiency with which some resource is being used.

The basic arithmetic of productivity is very simple—it is a ratio of some measure of output to some measure of input. One output-input measure, for example, with which every car owner is familiar, is miles per gallon of gasoline. This measure is used not as a gauge of the efficiency of the gasoline but as an indicator of the efficiency of the car's performance.

Illustrated here is one of the first principles of a productivity ratio. It does not necessarily represent the efficiency of the specific resource used in the input measure but rather the combined effect of a number of factors. Thus, miles per gallon of gasoline is a ratio which reflects the size and efficiency of the engine, speed, road conditions, traffic and traffic lights and other factors, as well as the efficiency of the gasoline itself. The latter is, of course, very important. The American car owner takes for granted that the gasoline he purchases will have octane ratings and quality standards on which he can depend for power and other performance. The accumulated technology, research, and experience of the petroleum refining companies are often forgotten and certainly are not explicitly measured when adding up "gallons of gasoline."

These observations are also true, in varying degree, of company productivity ratios which relate output to any one of the inputs such as labor, capital, or materials. Each ratio is influenced by the volume and quality of the other inputs employed and how effectively they are used. Output per man-hour, output per unit of capital, and output per unit of labor plus capital are all influenced by the volume of capital equipment, its stage of technological development, the quality and availability of materials, the scale of operations and rate of capacity utilization, organization and workflow, and other factors—as well as the very important contribution of the skill and attitude of the work force, including management.

It is very important to recognize this interplay of factors which may affect the rate of productivity. If the rate of increase in output per unit of some resource, any resource, appears to be lagging behind the industry's performance or behind some expected standard, the causes of that lag are usually not found in the ratio.

Confusion about the meaning of productivity often arises because different measures are possible and because different compilers or users often claim that there is only one "true" measure (their own, naturally) and the others are somehow inferior or of secondary importance. This guide will concentrate on one form of measurement—output per man-hour. Other types of measures will be reviewed briefly, but this is not to cast any one measure in an inferior or superior position. Output per man-hour is chosen because it serves many useful purposes; it is an important factor in estimating future labor requirements, it is related to wages and labor costs and to wage and price control programs, and is in demand. It is also recommended by the author as a measure which is more easily understood than the alternatives.

The intensity of interest in productivity is often associated with events of the business cycle or with long term developments in social and economic affairs. These events may also have some influence on the kind of productivity ratio most in demand or receiving the most attention from management, labor, government, and the general public.

When unemployment is high, concern over the labor displacement effects of technology (automation in these modern times) heightens the interest in productivity, especially as measured by output per unit of labor input. During periods of inflation the relationship of productivity to costs becomes a more paramount issue. The same is true of the individual firm whenever its costs are rising to the detriment of profits. Domestic competition and inroads of foreign competition bring greater attention to unit costs and to productivity as an important element of those costs.

The economic stabilization program which went into effect in the late summer of 1971 and the Economic Stabilization Act of April 1972 brought the interest in productivity and its measurement to new heights. By virtue of legislation and guidelines set by the Price Commission, attention to productivity measurement became more than a matter of interest; it became a matter of necessity. In this case, output per man-hour was used as the guiding productivity ratio.

Various types of ratios in use at the plant level are often called productivity ratios. These include operating ratios, performance ratios, labor ratios, and so on. They often fail to meet one important criterion of a productivity ratio, namely, that the output and the input be expressed in constant terms over the selected time period.

One type of "productivity" ratio that is sometimes used in labor-management sharing plans is payrolls as a percent of sales. This ratio can be very useful as an element in sharing plan formulas, but it fails as a measure of productivity trend unless, over time, the payrolls and the value of sales are deflated by an appropriate wage index and price index, respectively. Otherwise, the ratio can decline (i.e., improve) because prices are raised (and profits increased), or because there is a shift to higher valued products (see Chapter 3). It can increase if wages are raised.

Technical difficulties of measurement also arise as the outputs of an enterprise or an industry become more diversified and complex and as old products disappear and new ones take their place. A common and difficult problem to solve occurs where products do not completely disappear but are modified from one year (or less) to the next. As one moves from the production of goods to the production of service, the concepts of output become more difficult to comprehend and to define, and the difficulties of measurement are compounded.

It is not likely that any firm will have in its accounting records the kind of detail needed for absolutely precise measurements of productivity, nor is a firm likely to engage in the expense of setting up and maintaining such records. But that is not necessary. The measurements obtained, for the establishment or for entire industries, need not have the penny precision of a balance sheet. What is important is that the measures yield a reasonably accurate picture of what is taking place and that the user not be misled by small, fractional, and insignificant differences in performance.

This guide book will begin with simple types of production and move through more complex production situations. Examples will be given to illustrate the methods of calculation. The feasibility of these methods will depend on their relationship to existing cost-accounting procedures or on the ability of the firm to modify its accounting procedures without incurring excessive costs.

Before turning to detailed definitions and the exposition of techniques, let us again state the concept and formulation. We begin with the simple and common measure:

Output per unit of input = Output ÷ Input = Productivity

It is often useful to think about this measure in the inverse form:

Input ÷ Output = Unit resource requirements

This form may be particularly convenient for some of the most complex calculations.

The chapters which follow deal, for the most part, with the measurement of productivity trends—measures which can be used to evaluate the firm's progress, including comparison with industry trends. The measurement of the level of productivity is dealt with only briefly (in Chapter 3) in the context of industry comparisons.

CHAPTER 2

Man-Hours and Labor Productivity

In the previous chapter it was noted that productivity and costs were related but not equivalent. Many companies regularly compute and maintain an array of information dealing with unit costs, often referred to as "operating ratios." These may include payrolls per dollar of sales, value added per employee, material costs as a percent of value of output or sales, capital costs per dollar of production or sales, and other ratios. Each of these ratios is composed of two basic elements, the price of the resource (or input), and the quantity of the resource used (input) in relation to the output. The latter relationship expresses the productivity concept.

The ratio "payrolls per dollar of sales" is a useful one to illustrate how we move from a current operating ratio to a productivity ratio. Payrolls are composed of an earnings rate (the "price" of labor) and the quantity of labor. Dollars of sales are composed of a price per unit and a quantity of units. Both wages and prices are usually expressed in current dollars.

The operating ratio "payrolls per dollar of sales" is generally used in analysis of the firm's financial operations. A first step in cost-accounting analysis is to express sales in constant dollars or in physical units where that is possible. A second step is to adjust volume of goods sold to a production figure by making appropriate inventory adjustments; sales and labor input for a particular period may not match because of accumulation of inventory or its depletion at a later date.

A third step is to decompose payrolls into wage and salary rates and into quantity of labor. We now have the units needed for the common measure of productivity—quantity of output and quantity of labor input. It may be noted that this process of decomposition also provides the manager or cost accountant with information for studying labor costs.

Employment to Be Included

The use of the term "labor" sometimes carries with it the connotation of unskilled work. More frequently it is thought of as comprising the "production" or blue-collar work force and excluding the white-collar component. This is unfortunate since all employees make some contribution, direct or indirect, to the firm's output, and the man-hours and the wages of all employees must enter into the calculation of costs and ultimately of price.

It is desirable that the firm's measure of productivity should cover the hours of all its employees, including the janitor and the president. In addition to the reasons already given, this may be quite important when making comparisons with other firms or with industry as a whole. Because of differences in technology, in management concepts, or for other reasons, not all firms are organized in exactly the same way. Consequently, some firms have a different proportion of production or direct workers to total employment than others. Production-worker productivity may therefore vary from one company to another even when all-employee productivity is the same.

It may also be desirable for management analysis purposes to develop measures for smaller components of the work force. These will depend on the structure of the firm. In addition to a measure covering all employees, some possible subdivisions are:

All employees less:
> Outside salesmen
> Research and development employees

Production workers
> Total
> Direct
> Indirect

The manager who wishes to examine and evaluate the trend

of labor cost and labor usage can divide his firm's labor force into whatever other components he deems useful for analysis.

At this point it is necessary to draw a distinction among work measurement, productivity, and labor requirements ratios.

We have used the term "labor productivity" to reflect a ratio of a firm's total output to total employment. That same output can also be related to major components of the work force, such as output per production worker. As the labor component becomes smaller and smaller, however, output per unit of labor input becomes less and less meaningful because the small cadre of workers included are involved in only a small part of the production process. The inverse ratio, e.g., indirect workers per unit of output, may be a useful indicator of changing indirect labor requirements (or in some cases of wasteful build-up of overhead).

Work measurement commonly relates some phase of the firm's output to the labor time required for the particular production phase—subassemblies per man-hour in the subassembly department; pages (or lines) typed per typist hour. Insufficient attention to these work measures may lead to poor overall productivity; on the other hand, too much attention can lead to oversight of unnecessary activities.

Man-Hours Worked or Hours Paid for

A simple count of employment is usually not the best labor-input measure to use for productivity because it does not reflect the changes in labor input that are brought about by changes in the work week or in leave. It is much preferable to use man-hours as the labor-input component.

Two types of man-hour measures might be used to measure a firm's productivity, and both types are, in fact, used in government productivity statistics. The two types are "hours paid for" and "hours worked."

"Hours paid for" include all hours worked by employees plus hours not worked but paid for, including vacations, holidays, sick leave, jury duty, and any other paid leave. This hours measure has three possible advantages:

1. It is a measure of the total man-hours a firm must pay for in order to obtain a given volume of output at any given time.

2. Data on hours paid for may be more readily available from the personnel and payroll record system currently used by the firm; these records often do not provide an accounting for paid absences, particularly for workers paid on an annual, rather than an hourly, basis.

3. Most of the published information on hourly earnings is based on hours paid for. If the productivity index is to be compared with average earnings, it should be conceptually compatible, i.e., also based on man-hours paid for.

The greatest disadvantage of an hours-paid-for measure is that it is affected in different ways by different changes in work and leave practices. If the workweek is increased by overtime or decreased by a reduction in the scheduled hours of work, the weekly and annual hours paid for will be increased or decreased in proportion. On the other hand, if vacation, holiday, or other paid leave time is increased (or reduced), hours paid for are not affected by such changes. Thus, these two ways of granting additional leisure time—reduced workweek and increased paid leave—have a different impact on the count of hours paid for and consequently on output per man-hour paid for. The difference in the productivity indicator is merely an accounting difference and not a real one.

A preferred labor input is "hours worked," although this designation is subject to misinterpretation and sometimes to ridicule. An alternative title is "plant hours" (or establishment hours) a term used by the Bureau of the Census of the U.S. Department of Commerce. This measure covers all hours at the plant (establishment) including coffee breaks, rest periods, downtime, and other times within the scheduled hours whether employees are actually "working" or not. It excludes all leaves, whether paid or unpaid.

One of the major advantages of a measure of hours at work is that it reflects all changes in leave practices in the same way. If hours at work are reduced by a shorter week, by vacations, or by more holidays, the annual hours at work will reflect all three types of reductions. It is for this reason that hours at work is preferred for the measurement of productivity.

Information on hours at work is generally available for a substantial proportion of the employees, including many of those who are paid on a weekly rather than an hourly basis, because many of them are covered by state or federal wage and hour laws which require that records be kept. Records for professional, executive, and other employees, on the other hand, do not show overtime or temporary absence from the office, so information on their hours of work is not available. Estimates of those hours may be made by adjusting scheduled hours on the basis of known practices or of the trends in average hours of those for whom records are kept. Use of scheduled hours minus vacations and holidays is also an acceptable practice.

Changes in output per man-hour are often compared with changes in average hourly earnings or compensation. When this comparison is made the man-hour figures used in each of the ratios should be compatible; they should both be based on hours paid for or both based on hours at work. Table 1 shows the difference in compensation per hour paid for and per hour at work.

Table 1.   Computation of Compensation per Man-Hour

	Total	Paid leave	At the establishment
	(1)	(2)	(3)
A. Annual hours	20,800	1,300	19,500
B. Annual compensation [1]	$104,000	—	—
C. Compensation per man-hour [2]	$5.00	—	$5.33 1/3

[1] Includes wages, contributions to retirement, sick leave, unemployment, and other funds (public or private), and vacation and other leave pay.

[2] Compensation per hour paid for equals total compensation (Line B, Column 1) divided by total hours (Line A, Column 1). Compensation per establishment hour equals total compensation (Line B, Column 1) divided by establishment hours (Line A, Column 3).

The previous discussion has dealt with a counting of man-hours without differentiation by quality or skill. This is a useful measure for examining the trends in the use of a quantity of employment and is directly comparable with the industry productivity measures published by the U.S. Government.

It is also possible to prepare, if management is interested, a measure which takes account of the changing skill requirements of employment, known as a weighted man-hour index. It is simple in concept but may be difficult to prepare, depending on payroll and accounting systems. Procedures for preparing this kind of measure are covered in Chapter 6.

Arithmetic Examples of Basic Ratios and Index Numbers

When calculating percentage changes, it is usually simpler to think in terms of dividing the actual change by the base-period level (or ratio). In this guidebook, however, we will usually be dealing with calculations of index numbers, from which percentage changes are easily obtained. An index number is merely the percentage change added to or subtracted from 100. It can also be calculated directly from the basic data.

Most of the time the discussions and explanations will be in terms of first calculating an index of output and an index of man-hours (input) and then utilizing these two indexes to compute the productivity index. There are two reasons for this approach: (1) It is usually easier to perform the steps of calculation in this manner. (2) The method helps to provide a "family" of related statistics useful for analysis.

Index numbers have several advantages. They can be used to calculate or convert to other indexes. Percentage changes can easily be derived from them. They lend themselves to charting of trend lines. They can often be compared with government statistics. Industry productivity figures, for example, produced by the Bureau of Labor Statistics, are published in the form of annual indexes.[1] The BLS also usually computes and publishes average annual rates of change. The latter is a useful kind of average when comparing changes over two or more unequal time periods.

Annual percentage changes in establishment productivity can be compared directly with industry percentage changes. However, if indexes are compared the two sets must both be on the same "base,"

---

[1] *Indexes of Output Per Man-Hour, Selected Industries,* published annually by Bureau of Labor Statistics, U.S. Department of Labor, Washington, D. C.

i.e., calculated from the same base year.[2] Conversions to different reference base years are easily made. (For those interested in the algebra of conversion, see Appendix II.)

The computation of index numbers requires that some time period be chosen as the "base period." Usually this period is a year, but some care needs to be exercised so that the period chosen is not an abnormal one. It may be argued that there is no such thing as a "normal" year, but it is desirable, for example, not to use as a base a period which includes a major strike, or has a substantially atypical high, or low, volume of output.

The "formulas" for calculating productivity indexes are as follows:

(1) Direct
Index of Productivity = Productivity in current year,
                                                        divided by
                                 Productivity in base year.
                                 Times 100

(2) Indirect
Index of Productivity = Index of Output, divided by
                                 Index of man-hours. Times 100

In the various examples which appear in this booklet, some of the figures used may not appear to reflect the "real world," but this is done in an attempt to keep the arithmetic simple.

The data presented in Table 2 are intended to illustrate the development not only of basic simple productivity ratios but also of related ratios and index numbers. Figures are shown for units of output, without defining or explaining how they are derived. That will be done in Chapter 3. The data also indicate the kind of analytical information that can be available and helpful to department heads, managers, superintendents, and other levels of supervision. The table presents an array of statistics that are useful for analyzing employment costs and other trends in a fairly comprehensive manner. This same array of data can be developed for total employment or for components of the firm's work force.

---

[2] There also may be differences if different *weight* base years are used. This is a more complicated technical point which may sometimes affect the comparability of the two sets of indexes. For a more detailed discussion, see Chapter 6.

Table 2.   Calculating Simple Ratios and Indexes

Item	Base Period	Second Period	
		Amount	Index [1]
	(1)	(2)	(3)
Basic Data			
1. Output, units	100,000	126,000	126.0
2. Hours	20,000	21,000	105.0
3. Compensation	$ 80,000	$102,900	128.6
Ratios			
4. Output per man-hour (Line 1 ÷ Line 2)	5.0	6.0	120.0
5. Compensation per hour (Line 3 ÷ Line 2)	$4.00	$4.90	122.5
6. Unit employment costs (Line 3 ÷ Line 1) or (Line 5 ÷ Line 4)	$ .80	$ .81 2/3	102.1

[1] Indexes equal [Col. (2) ÷ Col. (1)] × 100. They may also be derived, as shown in lines 4, 5, and 6, by dividing one index by another.

It may first be noted that output rose 26 percent in the period covered by these data. That increase was attained with only a 5-percent increase in total man-hour input. Most of the gain in output was achieved by increases in labor productivity, i.e., by a 20-percent gain in output per man-hour. (Remembering, as noted in Chapter 1, that this increase might have been attained by use of more or better capital equipment, managerial organization, skill and effort of the work force, or other factors.)

Further evaluation of the firm's productivity performance cannot be made without more information. On the face of it, a 20-percent increase in labor productivity with a 26-percent increase in output is "good" performance. However, it would help to know how the firm has performed in past periods and how its record compares with that of the industry of which it is a part.

The employer paid a 22.5-percent increase in wages, salaries, and supplements during this period, but most of it was counterbalanced by the 20-percent gain in labor productivity, so unit employment costs rose only 2.1 percent.

From the workers' point of view, they more than shared in the firm's productivity increase, either by promotion to higher skilled jobs or by a general wage increase. Their gain in real income cannot be evaluated without knowing what happened to consumer prices during the period.

CHAPTER 3

The Measurement of Plant Output

This chapter deals primarily with measurement of output trends as a component of the rate of growth of productivity. Later in the chapter there will be a brief discussion about measures of the level of output as they relate to attempts to measure the actual productivity ratio at any given point in time.

Measuring the Trend of Output

For the plant which produces one product month after month, even year after year, measurement is very simple. The number of units produced during the period are counted. The sum for the current period is divided by the sum for the base period to obtain an output index.

Even in a plant which produces a variety of products, the units can be counted and the simple sum used as the measure of output if the specifications of each unit remain unchanged and if exactly the same proportions of units are produced from one time period to the next.

Cases of both types are rare. More commonly a firm produces a variety of products; sometimes they are gradually modified as time passes; sometimes new models are introduced as old ones are dropped. We will try to proceed from the relatively simple to the more complex measurement systems.

15

The Principle of Equivalents

The basic principle to be kept in mind in developing a system of output and productivity measurement is that all units produced by the firm are related to each other, more or less. If it is possible to place a "value" on one unit, then it should be possible to "value" other units produced. The values of the units should be conceptually equivalent to each other in a way which meets the basic objective of developing an output measure to be used for productivity ratios.

Dollar Value

All commodities and services, except for government services, are eventually equated to each other in the market place in the form of dollar value. All final products of the firm are similarly valued, that is, they have a selling price. It might be said that a dollar's worth of Product A is equivalent to a dollar's worth of Product B. Perhaps this is so for market purposes, but it may not be the most useful equivalent for productivity measurement in the firm.

The selling price of a commodity is influenced by several factors: cost of materials, labor, overhead, allocated capital depreciation, and markup or profit. When the first of these factors, cost of materials, is roughly in the same proportion for each of the final outputs of the firm, its inclusion in the output measure will introduce no serious bias or distortion. Sometimes, however, there is a substantial variation in the cost of materials for different products made by the same firm. This can occur because different raw materials are used or because components with different degrees of fabrication are purchased.

Let us assume a fictional sweater factory that makes only two types of sweaters, identical in every respect except that one is made of wool and the other of orlon (Table 3). Woolen sweaters, with higher cost raw materials, are more expensive than orlon sweaters. The factory produces 100 sweaters of each type in Period 1, but the consumers switch to the cheaper sweater so more orlon sweaters and fewer woolen sweaters are manufactured in Period 2.

Table 3.   Output and Productivity Calculation Using Value of Output

	Period 1			Period 2		
	Wool	Orlon	Total	Wool	Orlon	Total
Number of sweaters	100	100	200	50	150	200
Cost of yarn	$ 400	$ 200	$ 600	$ 200	$ 300	$ 500
Labor	200	200	400	100	300	400
Other costs and profits	400	400	800	200	600	800
Total value	$1,000	$ 800	$1,800	$ 500	$1,200	$1,700
Man-hours	50	50	100	25	75	100
Value per sweater	$10.00	$ 8.00	$ 9.00	$10.00	$18.00	$ 8.50
Dollar output per man-hour	$20.00	$16.00	$18.00	$20.00	$16.00	$17.00

In this fictional factory, each type of sweater requires the same volume of labor in its manufacture; these unit man-hour requirements remain unchanged from period one to period two. Yet labor productivity, as measured by value per man-hour, declines for the plant as a whole from $18 to $17 because of the shift to a higher relative volume of sweaters made of the lower cost orlon yarn.

Value Added

The influence of material costs can be removed by using a measure of output called value added, which is the difference between total cost or value and the value of materials purchased. It reflects cost of labor, capital depreciation, taxes, and profit markup. The value component markup may be affected by factors quite unrelated to the production process. Some commodities are produced and sold to "round out" a line of merchandise; the price on a given day, month, or year may be determined more by competitive factors than by production costs.

Constant-Dollar Value or Value Added

Both types of dollar value measures—total value (cost or price) and value added—may be affected by price changes. If prices rise, total value will rise even if nothing else changes, so resultant productivity indexes will show an unreal increase. If different products are subject to different pricing over time, this differential will also have a spurious and undesirable effect on the resultant output and productivity measures. So if value measurement systems are used they must be in constant prices.

Constant-dollar values are obtained by deflation or use of constant weights. For deflation the firm must have a price index available which reflects the pricing of its own mix of products; national price indexes are likely to be inapplicable to any specific firm.

If value added is used, then the so-called double deflation method is employed. Price indexes are required for the value of output and for the cost of materials. Each is separately deflated, and the deflated values are subtracted one from the other to obtain deflated value added. This deflation process can be applied to each product separately or to the total value of products and materials. In the latter case the price index must be an adequate representation (sample) of the totality of products.

It is likely that the firm which is sophisticated enough in its statistical techniques to maintain the kinds of price indexes just described will not need an explanation of price index construction and of deflation. However, the section on materials in Chapter 6 has an illustration of both.

Constant-dollar values can also be obtained by multiplying the number of units produced in each period by a constant-dollar weight, i.e., by the unit price in a base period. The techniques of weighting, whether by unit cost, unit price, or unit value added, are the same for each, and the same as for the preferred weights, unit man-hours, described in the next section.

The Preferred Output Measure—Man-Hour Equivalents

There are various kinds of ratios which are quite familiar to the average firm; they include cost per unit of output, cost or profit as a percent of sales, and ratio of payrolls to total costs or to value of shipments. These are all useful operating ratios, but they deal with dollar value, which can be affected by shifts among products or by price changes, as previously described. What we seek is some measure of the change in resources utilized for the production of physical quantities of goods—number of sweaters, tons of steel. However, we cannot add number of orlon sweaters to number of wool sweaters, or tons of carbon steel rods to tons of alloyed sheet steel.

We return to the principle of equivalents, not dollar equivalents but some unit which expresses the physical value of the product. Man-hours are the most appropriate unit for developing a measure of the physical output of the firm. Such a measure is not affected by shifts in the proportions of goods manufactured, by differences in the market value of products, or by changes in prices.

The measures we will derive are based on the principle of equating all products in accordance with the number of man-hours required to make each product at a certain time period. In this system one hour of carbon steel equals one hour of alloy steel; one hour of orlon sweater equals one hour of wool sweater. (In fact, one hour of steel equals one hour of sweater; any two products can be equated.) At the end of any time period the data produced will permit the following kind of productivity analysis:

The goods produced during this period required Y hours of employee time (direct or total). Production of this same complex of products during the base period would have required X hours. Therefore, the index of unit labor requirements is $(Y \div X) \, 100$; the index of productivity equals $(X \div Y) \, 100$.

The development of this system of measures requires that the man-hour requirements be available (or be constructed or estimated) for each product for a base period. For subsequent periods, only total hours, for all products combined, are needed; detail by product is not required. However, new detailed information for each product will need to be developed periodically as new products enter the production line and old products are phased out. When significant changes occur in volume of different products, the relative unit labor requirements are also likely to change significantly. The use of a set of weights for too long a period of time under such circumstances can lead to meaningless combinations of products. It has been found that for purposes of developing industry productivity measures revision of the man-hour weights is desirable about every 10 years. At the company level it may be desirable to revise the weights more frequently.

Changes in a firm's "make or buy" practices may also affect the relative input requirements for different products while the gross output measures are not similarly affected.

Our first illustrative example is a firm which manufactures three products in each of two different periods. The product specifications remain the same, but the fraction of total production accounted for by each product changes.

Table 4.   Output Per Man-Hour Computations Using
Unit Man-Hour Weights
(Products Remain Unchanged)

| | Base Period | | | Period T | | |
Product	Units	Man-Hours Per Unit	Weighted Units (2) × (3)	Units	Man-Hours	Weighted Units (5) × (3)
(1)	(2)	(3)	(4)	(5)	(6)	(7)
A	4	5.0	20	12		60
B	5	4.0	20	5		20
C	10	2.0	20	20		40
Total	XX	60 [1]	60	XX	90 [1]	120

[1] Total actual hours, usually obtainable from payroll records.

In the example in Table 4 it took five hours to manufacture a unit of Product A in the base period, four hours for a unit of B, and two hours for a unit of C. Therefore, one unit of A was equivalent to 2.5 units of C; one unit of B was equivalent to 2.0 units of C. The ratios 2.5, 2.0 and 1.0 can be used as weights, but it is usually more convenient to use the actual base-period unit manhours, as shown in the example.

During the base period the firm produced a total of 19 units of A, B, and C. By using man-hour weights (i.e., the man-hour equivalents) we can say that the firm produced 60 weighted units of output—or the equivalent of 60 man-hours of output. The number of hours expended was also equal to 60, which is as it should be for the base period. (Overhead man-hours are assumed to be allocated.) Sixty (weighted) units divided by 60 man-hours times 100 gives an output per man-hour index of 100 for the base period.

In Period T there were 37 units of Products A, B, and C. We know from the firm's payroll or other records that a total of 90 hours was spent in the firm to produce those units. The unit man-hours for each product are not shown separately in Period T, may not be known, and are not needed. All we need to know is the total number of hours (90) in Period T.

If we multiply the number of units produced in Period T (Column 5) by the base-year weight (unit man-hours required in Base Period as shown in Column 3), we obtain the number of weighted units for Period T (Column 7). This calculation says, "If we had produced this year's mix of products at base-year pro-ductivity rates, it would have taken 120 hours." It is the weighted output figure for Period T.

We now have the data available to calculate the productivity change, a step which can be taken in any of several ways:

(1) The actual hours (90) in Period T divided by the weighted output (120) times 100 yields an index of 75. This index says that there was a reduction of 25 percent in unit man-hour requirements.

(2) The inverse calculation, weighted output (120) divided by man-hours (90), is an index of output per man-hour. This index, 133.3, shows a productivity gain of 33-1/3 percent. Note that, when large percentage changes occur, the percentage decrease in unit man-hours will always be smaller than the percentage increase in output per man-hour.

(3) Indexes of output and man-hours are calculated:

Index of output	$= (120 \div 60) \, 100$	$= 200$
Index of man-hours	$= (90 \div 60) \, 100$	$= 150$
Index of output per man-hour	$= (200 \div 150) \, 100$	$= 133.3$

The use of method (3) permits the firm to follow its year-to-year (or month-to-month) changes in both output and productivity. Comparison of the two changes facilitates analysis of the production developments in the firm.

New Products

We come now to more complex problems of measurement and to situations where the measurement system is less precise because it requires assumptions or estimates.

Quite often the specifications of a product or products are modified. Sometimes a brand new product is introduced. This means that there is no base-period man-hour equivalent for the new or modified product, since it did not exist in the base period. A base-period equivalent needs to be estimated. This can be done in various ways, depending on the kinds of cost-accounting records kept by the firm. Remember—even if there is some imprecision in the estimate for this one product, it is not likely to have a great impact on the overall measure.

If the firm keeps detailed records of unit man-hours for each product on a current basis, the best and simplest method is:

(1) Obtain unit man-hours for the new product for the current period.

(2) Obtain a ratio of unit hours for the new product to unit hours of an old product, preferably some "standard" product.

(3) Apply this ratio to the unit hours of the old product in the base period to obtain estimated base-period unit hours for the new product.

If cost-accounting records do not furnish unit man-hours but do furnish unit cost figures currently, follow steps (1) and (2), using unit costs. Apply the ratio obtained in step (2) to a base-year man-hour figure as in step (3). If neither unit hours nor unit costs are available, use unit values.

Let us assume that the plant in Table 4 introduces a new product D. The calculations would be as shown in Table 5.

Table 5. Output Per Man-Hour Computations
(Introduction of a New Product)

Product	Units	Base Period Man-Hours per Unit	Base Period Weighted Units (2) × (3)	Units	Period T Man-Hours	Period T Weighted Units (5) × (3)
(1)	(2)	(3)	(4)	(5)	(6)	(7)
A	4	5.0	20	12		60
B	5	4.0	20	5		20
C	10	2.0	20	20		40
D	—	6.0 [1]	—	5		30
Total	XX	60 [2]	60	XX	112.5 [2]	150

[1] Estimated. Used only to calculate weighted "D" units for Column 7.
[2] Total actual hours.

For Period T:

Index of output	$= (150 \div 60)\ 100$	$= 250$
Index of man-hours	$= (112.5 \div 60)\ 100$	$= 187.5$
Index of output per man-hour	$= (250 \div 187.5)\ 100$	$= 133.3$
Index of unit man-hour requirements	$= (187.5 \div 250)\ 100$	$= 75.0$

Note that the index of output per man-hour is exactly the same as that in Table 4. This is a result of the fact that the method of estimating base-year unit man-hours for the new product implicitly assumes that the productivity trend for that product from the base period to the current period is equal to the average productivity change for all of the old products.

There is a caution to be noted in estimating the man-hours for a new product. When a new product is first introduced it may undergo a period of testing and debugging. During that period its unit hours and unit costs may be very high and quite atypical of its unit man-hour requirements and unit costs after the break-in period. If its atypical break-in requirements are used as the basis for extrapolating back to a base-period unit man-hour estimate and retained at this level for future periods, the resulting productivity estimates for those periods may be seriously distorted. It is, therefore, desirable that a "normal" production run be used as the basis for estimating.

If cost or value figures are not available currently or are believed to distort the physical concept for reasons previously discussed or for other reasons, some less precise estimate may be used. It is suggested that the industrial engineer, plant superintendent, cost accountant, or other person knowledgeable about the plant operations may be able to develop an approximation, following the principle of equivalents as previously described.

Multiplicity of Specification Changes

It is not unusual in some industries for a plant to make a variety of products which do not remain standard from year to year and for which there are a variety of specification changes. Three alternative methods of calculation are suggested for this type of plant.

Method 1. One can treat each altered product as a new product and follow the procedures described in the preceding section under "New Products."

Method 2. Sometimes the new or modified product is substantially identical to the "old" product but some of the components (final design, cabinetry, engine size, etc.) are modified. In this case we try, as closely as we can, to follow a system which:

(a) Identifies and establishes a major segment of the final product as being identical from one period to the next.

(b) Treats the modifications separately as "old" and "new" products.

(c) Drops the old products (components) from the current year's calculation, and adds the new products (components, modifications) to the current year's calculation.

The procedures then are as described under "New Products." (See also Chapter 4.)

Method 3. Over long periods of time there is a greater likelihood of attrition in comparability of products. The shorter the time period, the more likely it is that comparability will be retained. For those plants with frequent and substantial changes in product it may be necessary to use a method which compares products only over adjacent "short" periods of time. This may be year to year or month to month (Table 6).

In this case, the "base year" changes every year. The "market basket" of products is comparable, strictly speaking, only between the two adjacent time periods.

Using this method we calculate a successive series of percentage changes in productivity for adjacent time periods. We then take the liberty of "linking" these percentage changes together over the entire time period we wish to have included in our measurement and analysis system.

For this method it is essential to have reasonably good estimates of the unit man-hours for each new product, or modification,
for each time period. (Or, if unit man-hours are not available,
unit labor costs, total unit cost, and unit value.) This requires a
more extensive and costly cost-accounting system. If the cost-
accounting system produces unit man-hour information for each
product or component for each period to be measured, it is possible to use what is known as current-year weighting.

The methods thus far employed have combined the various
products by equating them in terms of base-year weights. It is also
permissible to combine them with current-year weights—in this
case the output data for both the base year and current year are
combined with current-year weights. Under this method the weights,
obviously, change each year (or whatever other time period is used).

It may be noted that the use of base-year rather than current-
year weights might have very little impact on the final results or
matter a great deal. It depends on a number of factors: the difference in the weights for each product; the change in relative output
of the various products; the change in the proportionate weight of
each product.

Quite often, if the two time periods which are being compared
and for which calculations are being made are adjacent to each
other, the choice of weights is not likely to make a great deal of
difference. In this case the analyst's choice might be the one which
simplifies the calculating process. However, the method should be
consistent from period to period, since otherwise the series of
results may lose compatibility.

In Table 6 (page 26) we will use current-year weights. Product D is a second-period modification of Product C; Product E is
introduced in Period 3; Product B is discontinued in Period 3.

The table is generally self-explanatory, and one can follow the
system of calculation by tracing through the steps shown. But it
may be useful to highlight some of the stages of calculation.

1. For each pair of years "weighted units" are obtained by
   multiplying early-period units by the unit man-hours of the
   following period. That is why the total of weighted units

in Period 1 is different from the total for the base period as shown in Table 4, even though all other factors are the same.

2. Calculations are made for each pair of years—in detail and in computing year-to-year indexes. For each pair, the index for the early year is, in effect, a base-period index equal to 100. The indexes are then linked as shown in Part B.

Quality Change

A criticism frequently directed at index numbers of production and productivity, as well as of prices, is that they do not take account of quality change, whether it be improvement or deterio-

Table 6.   Linking for Frequent Product Changes

A. Detail

		Period 1				Period 2	
Product	No. Units	Man-Hours Per Unit [1]	Weighted Units (7) × (2)	Product	No. Units	Man-Hours Per Unit	Weighted Units (7) × (6)
(1)	(2)	(3)	(4)	(5)	(6)	(7)	(8)
A	4	5.0	18	A	6	4.5	27.0
B	5	4.0	20	B	4	4.0	16.0
C	10	2.0	18	C	12	1.8	21.6
D	—	—	—	D	12	.1	1.2
Total		60 [2]	56	Total		65.8 [2]	65.8

		Period 2				Period 3	
			(15) × (10)				(15) × (14)
(9)	(10)	(11)	(12)	(13)	(14)	(15)	(16)
A	6	4.5	26.4	A	6	4.4	26.4
B	4	4.0	16.0	B	—	4.0 [3]	—
C	12	1.8	20.4	C	14	1.7	23.8
D	12	.1	1.2	D	14	.1	1.4
E	—	—	—	E	6	3.1	18.6
Total		65.8 [2]	64.0	Total		70.2 [2]	70.2

[1] Unit man-hours for Period 1 not used in computations.
[2] Total actual hours.
[3] Estimated.

Table 6—Contd.
B. Calculation of Indexes and Percent Change

	Index Period 1	Index Period 2	Percent Change
Output	100	$(65.8 \div 56) \ 100 = 117.5$	17.5
Man-hours	100	$(65.8 \div 60) \ 100 = 109.7$	9.7
Output per man-hour	100	$(117.5 \div 109.67) \ 100 = 107.1$	7.1
Unit man-hours	100	$(109.67 \div 117.5) \ 100 = \ 93.3$	—6.7
	Period 2	Period 3	
Output	100	$(70.2 \div 64.0) \ 100 = 109.7$	9.7
Man-hours	100	$(70.2 \div 65.8) \ 100 = 106.7$	6.7
Output per man-hour	100	$(109.7 \div 106.7) \ 100 = 102.8$	2.8
Unit man-hours	100	$(106.7 \div 109.7) \ 100 = \ 97.3$	—2.7
	Period 1	Period 3	
Output	100	$(117.5 \times 109.7) \div 100 = 128.9$	28.9
Man-hours	100	$(109.7 \times 106.7) \div 100 = 117.0$	17.0
Output per man-hour	100	$(107.1 \times 102.8) \div 100 = 110.1$ [4]	10.1
Unit man-hours	100	$(93.3 \times 97.3) \div 100 = \ 90.8$ [5]	—9.2

[4] Also equal to $(128.9 \div 117.0) \ 100$. Small differences are due to rounding.
[5] Also equal to $(117.0 \div 128.9) \ 100$. Differences are due to rounding.

ration. Quite often, a change in quality is accompanied by a change in specification. In fact, quality change and specification change are practically synonymous.

When quality changes are directly observable as specification changes, they can be taken care of, in the output and productivity measures, as described in the preceding sections of this chapter.

This technique is essentially the same as that used by the Bureau of Labor Statistics in its price-index work to take account of the annual model changes in new cars. The automobile manufacturers provide the BLS with detailed information on deletions, additions, and modifications to the particular basic cars which are in the BLS sample. They also provide information on the relative (or actual) cost of each of the changes. The BLS then, in effect, revalues the old-year model by adding or subtracting the value of the changes, as appropriate, so that the old-year model is restructured in the image of the new-model car.

There are occasionally some types of quality improvement of benefit to the consumer which do not require any incremental input or cost by the producer. Such quality improvements represent a "utility" or "satisfaction" to the consumer, but no satisfactory measurement devices have been developed.

Levels of Productivity

This chapter has thus far dealt with the measurement of changes in productivity. Some firms may wish to compute a current productivity ratio, particularly for comparison with other firms. The difficulties here are often greater than those found in measuring changes in productivity, primarily because the comparability of outputs required for this purpose is usually not available. Differences between firms in the precise specifications of output or in valuations of different products may not have much impact on measurements of trends as long as the differences remain reasonably consistent. However, such differences might have a significant effect on productivity ratios calculated for a given point in time.

Some guidelines for computation and comparison are given in this section, together with some precautionary notes. The reader is warned, however, that there may be other traps and pitfalls on this route which are not specifically mentioned. Special problems often arise, depending on the nature of the product or the process, and the plant manager and analyst should be on the lookout for them. The exposition will be in terms of output per man-hour, but, of course, ratios with other inputs may be substituted.

Every four or five years the Bureau of the Census of the U.S. Department of Commerce conducts an extensive survey of all manufacturing establishments, the Census of Manufactures. (The rest of the private economy is surveyed less frequently.) In that survey a great volume of information is collected from establishments and published in the form of voluminous industry and product statistics. The Census Bureau also conducts an annual survey in which somewhat less information is collected and published. The annual survey is based on a smaller number of establishments; all establishments of 250 or more employees are asked to report (although a few may not), and a sample of firms with fewer than 250 employees are solicited for reports.

There are about 65,000 manufacturing establishments which have reported to the Census Bureau and have a ready source of reference data in their files—a copy of the schedule submitted to the Census Bureau. These firms are in a position to undertake some calculations with relative ease for comparison with similar data for their own industry published by the Bureau of the Census.[1] Other firms wishing to make these comparisons will first have to compile some basic statistics.

The simplest ratio to compute would be value of production per man-hour. The limitations of this ratio have already been pointed out—it is highly influenced by the quantity and value of purchased materials. If there is considerable variation in the ratio of materials purchased to value of output, interfirm comparisons can be quite meaningless. If all firms tend to purchase the same proportionate quantities of materials, then this ratio is more meaningful.

A much better kind of ratio is value added per man-hour. It avoids the possibility of duplication which may exist because of interplant shipments. It also overcomes the major part of the noncomparability arising from different materials purchasing patterns, including make-or-buy practices.

A simple definition of value added is value of output (or shipments adjusted for inventory change) minus the cost of materials, supplies, containers, fuel, purchased electricity, and contract work. The Census Bureau also adds receipts for services rendered and value added by merchandising operations (the difference between the sales value and cost of merchandise sold without further manufacture, processing, or assembly).

The value-added-per-man-hour ratio can be a very useful one, but some precautions should be noted. There can be great variations in this ratio among establishments. The "best" 25 percent might have a ratio five times as high as the lowest 25 percent, on the average. Sometimes this difference reflects large differences in efficiency among the firms. Other factors, however, may be influential. Even among establishments in the same standard four-digit industrial classification, a wide variety of products may be manufactured. Some require more man-hours than do others. In such cases it may

---

[1] Census of Manufactures (1967) and Annual Survey of Manufactures, 1970.

be product rather than efficiency differences which cause the difference in the productivity ratio.

Other factors which may result in interplant differences are degree of specialization and size of establishment. Plants which specialize in the manufacture of one or a few products and/or which have large-scale operations are likely to have higher output-per-man-hour ratios than those which do not.

Computing productivity ratios which relate output to some measure of labor input also raises the question of whether the hours of all employees or only those of production workers should be used. It would be desirable to include all employees in order to minimize interfirm productivity differences that might simply reflect differences in the structure of the firm or in classification of workers. Hours of production workers for the industry as a whole are usually available from the Bureau of the Census or the Bureau of Labor Statistics. Hours of nonproduction (or office) workers are not and would have to be estimated. It should be noted that there may be substantial differences in the occupational mix of nonproduction workers among firms. In some cases salesmen may be included; in some firms there are research and development workers who do not contribute directly to current production; in some firms administrative and auxiliary personnel are on the payroll of the establishment, whereas in others, particularly multiplant companies, they may be located in a central headquarters. There is no neat, ideal solution to this question. It is probably advisable to compute two ratios, one based on production-worker hours and the other on all-employee hours.

The value added, which has been obtained by subtracting purchases from output, can be looked at as the sum of payrolls and profits plus other costs. In this sense, value added per man-hour is affected by wage and salary rates and by profitability. It would be helpful to make interfirm comparisons by some measure of physical output per man-hour, but the statistics for this purpose are just not available. There may be a few instances where industry associations collect and publish the required data, but they are rare. Moreover, different products must be combined with an appropriate set of weights which should be the same for the firm and the industry.

CHAPTER 4

The Job Shop

It would be misleading to say that measuring the trend of productivity in a job shop is just the same as and therefore no more difficult than measuring the trend in a plant which mass produces a wide variety of complex products. It is not so much that the job shop produces on order rather than for stock which makes measurement different and more difficult, but the fact that so many of the final outputs produced in one time period are different from those produced in the next time period. This lack of product uniformity over time makes it quite difficult to establish comparability of output measures. And yet it is possible to develop productivity trend estimates for the job shop by following the principle of measurement enunciated in Chapter 3—namely, one must develop a system of equivalents.

It may not be possible to prescribe a formula for measuring output and productivity which can be directly and exactly applied to any specific job shop. There are, however, several ways in which the problem can be approached and a solution found.

We start with the fact that the final products of the shop differ from one another in some degree—they are sufficiently different that we cannot compare the time and cost of producing a product in the current period with the time and cost for the same product in some previous period. At the same time, there is some limitation to the variety and diversity of products, and there is likely to be some commonality among the products. The output of a particular job shop is not completely random or universal. The shop which engages in fabrication of stairs, fire escapes, and other architectural

31

metal work is not likely to be engaged in the manufacture of pumps and compressors, nor is either type of shop likely to be making motors and generators.

The Method of Equivalents

The shop manager should seek to find a common element among the products of his shop. Is there a basic component, common to all the outputs, which is then modified or added to in some way to satisfy customer orders? If so, then the common component is established as a base for measurement, and all the other additions and modifications are equated to that base. This is the kind of technique that is used to handle the annual model changes in automobiles.

Detailed specifications are obtained for each car, and structural changes are added or subtracted to determine the change in value. For example, when exhaust-emission-control devices are added, the value of the device is added to the basic value of the car. If a clock was standard on a model and becomes optional, its value is subtracted from the value of the newer model.

Job shops differ, of course, in their degree of vertical integration. Some shops perform only a few operations; others run the gamut from processing of raw materials through subassembly to assembly of the final product. The degree of integration is also relevant to the components and base unit. It is necessary to examine and evaluate the degree to which fabrication and assembly are performed on the basic unit and on the supplement, whether in the shop or outside the shop. If, for example, the supplement is fabricated and subassembled by a supplier, a substantial part of its value is a result of supplier efforts. If, on the other hand, the basic unit is primarily fabricated and subassembled in the shop, a substantial part of its value is a result of shop efforts. The relationship between value of output and input requirements is therefore not compatible as between the components and the base unit.

The use of dollar value presents a problem similar to the one described in Chapter 3 on the measurement of the value of different final products. The use of dollar values (unit price) for components leads to productivity measurements which reflect shifts among components with different values per man-hour. That is why the preferred procedure is to equate the basic component with the supplements in terms of man-hours, if the records of the company can provide sufficient data for this purpose. The problem should not be overblown. If man-hour requirements per dollar of value are roughly the same for the different components, the use of either unit value or man-hours (as weights) will yield similar results. Identical results are obtained when unit man-hours and value are exactly proportional.

The simple addition and subtraction of supplements to a basic unit to form two products is shown in Table 7. Both products (models) use the same basic unit with a value of 200 (man-hours or dollars). The old model includes supplements C and E; the new model uses four different supplements, A, B, D, and F.

Table 7.   Change in Value Between Old and New Models

Unit	Value of Old Model	Value of New Model
Basic	200	200
Supplements		
A	—	20
B	—	10
C	15	—
D	—	25
E	5	—
F	—	20
Total	220	275

Table 8 illustrates how the values of several different models can be combined without necessarily determining the value (in man-hours or dollars) of each model. In both periods there were 10 products, each with the basic unit at value of 200. In Period 1, there were five units with the A supplement at a base-period value of 20, eight units with supplement C at a base-period value of 15, and so on. All of the component (or supplement) units are weighted by their base-year value to obtain weighted value of total output.

Table 8.   Change in Output: Basic Unit Plus Supplements

Unit	Period 1			Period 2	
	Value	Number	Weighted	Number	Weighted
	(1)	(2)	(1)$\times$(2) (3)	(4)	(1)$\times$(4) (5)
Basic	200	10	2000	10	2000
Supplements					
A	20	5	100	8	160
B	10	—	—	10	100
C	15	8	120	2	30
D	25	2	50	8	200
E	5	10	50	2	10
F	20	4	80	7	140
Total			2400		2640

Index = 2640 ÷ 2400 = 110
Change in output = 10 percent

In Period 2 there were also 10 products with the base unit at value 200 but with different combinations of supplemental components, eight of A, two of C, and so on. A new component B was made in Period 2. B therefore had no real value in Period 1, but a theoretical value is computed by relating the new component's value in Period 2 to the value of the basic unit in the same period. That proportion is applied to the value of the basic unit in Period 1 to obtain a base-period value for the new component.

In some shops there may be groups of products, each group having a common base. The system of measurement is the same as that just described for the shop which produces a variety of products, all having one common base. A measure of output needs to be developed for each group as in Table 8, and the groups are then combined in exactly the same way that products are combined.

In still a third type of shop there may be no basic element common to the final product or groups of products. The principle of measurement, however, is the same—that of establishing equivalents. It may be possible to find some unit or component of output (a base) and relate other units or components to it.

This measurement by equivalents does not come easily or automatically. Firms which have comprehensive cost accounting systems may be able to establish equivalents relatively easily. If not, a one-time study is required.

In either case the values need to be redetermined periodically as technology and other factors change. The frequency of redetermination will vary, depending on how frequently and how radically the products or production factors change. Every five or eight years may be sufficient in some cases; yearly changes, requiring the linking method, may be necessary in others.

Outputs Versus Operation

In the preceding discussion we have measured the output of the job shop by counting, in an appropriate way, each of the various products or components produced in the shop. Some cost accounting systems may provide detailed information about operations (welding, forming, assembly) rather than about a unit of product. Such information might be used as a proxy for output but this method has a potentially serious inherent flaw, and it is not recommended. When technology changes or new equipment is utilized or a new production system is introduced, the operation changes and may no longer be comparable with the previous one. In fact, the operation may no longer be necessary and therefore will disappear from the accounting records. When this happens, the improvements in productivity may not show up in the productivity measure at all.

Multiple-Regression Accounting

There is a method of analysis used in the social and natural sciences to measure the results of the interaction of many variables. This technique is called "multiple-regression analysis." It may have potential for the job shop—indeed, for any type of firm. The method will not be described here in detail, but some fundamentals to indicate its possible use will be described. For those interested in pursuing the technique it is suggested that a statistician, econometrician, or someone else familiar with multiple-regression analysis be consulted.

This method of analysis requires that the following data be available: total man-hours for each final product; and the specifications (sub-units, components) of each final product. It is a variant of the principle of equivalents, but the major distinction, a very important one for record-keeping purposes, between this method and the others previously described is that it does not require an accounting of the man-hours (value) for each of the sub-units or components of the final product.

It should be noted that this method is not likely to produce results as precise as those of the standard methods. It can, however, produce results which are accurate enough for the manager to evaluate his firm's productivity progress, or lack of it. The degree of accuracy is related to the volume of production and degree of commonality among the components of the final product. For example, in the extreme and unlikely case where the final products are completely different from each other, the multiple-regression technique is inapplicable. In contrast, the results are likely to be very accurate for the shop with a large volume of output—several thousand units of final product—and where each component is used many times, even though not in all of the final products.

The method requires many tedious calculations. Computer facilities, captive or under contract, are highly desirable.

To illustrate the multiple-regression technique, let us assume a shop with 100 units of final output during a base period (month, quarter, year). No two of these are exactly alike, but many contain similar components. For each final unit of output we have a count of total direct hours. (Total hours, with indirect hours properly allocated, may also be used). For simplicity's sake, let us assume that 10 different components, A through J, are used in different combinations to make the 100 final units.

For each final unit there would be an equation which would look something like:

$$1 (A) + 1 (B) + 2 (C) = 80 \text{ Hours}$$

This says that it took 80 hours to produce a unit which included one component A, one B, and two C.

For other units the equations would be similar. For example:

$$1 (A) + 1 (C) + 2 (D) + 4(J) = 160 \text{ Hours}$$
$$1 (B) + 1 (C) + 2 (E) + 1 (G) + 3 (H) = 120 \text{ Hours}$$

These simple equations are weighted by number of units and summed. When this is done the sum of the man-hours should be equal to the total plant man-hours (all employees or direct, depending on what was included). Calculations are performed to solve the set of "simultaneous equations" and thus determine the respective values of the components A through J. The final result will look something like:

$$\text{Man-hours} = 5.2 + 24.0 \,(A) + 18.0 \,(B) + 12.3 \,(C) + 4.8 \,(D) + \ldots \ldots + .9J$$

The first number is a constant. The number next to each letter component is a factor to be multiplied by the number of components. A unit with one A, two C, and two D would require:

$$5.2 + 24.0 \,(1) + 18.0 \,(2) + 4.8 \,(2) =$$
$$5.2 + 24.0 + 36.0 + 9.6 = 74.8 \text{ Hours}$$

Suppose six months later the shop produced a unit with the components one A, two C, and two D and that it took 64 hours. We could calculate that there was a reduction of 10.8 hours in the time required for that unit or a productivity improvement of nearly 17 percent.

That is probably too simplistic a way of using the multiple-regression analysis. The better way is to substitute in the formula all of the components made during the period to be evaluated (a month, six months, a year) and then calculate the total plant man-hours that would be required, according to the formula. Compare this with actual total plant hours to obtain an indicator of the change in the plant's productivity. The individual product productivities may be calculated and might be useful, along with other information, to help the manager isolate sources of low productivity, but the statistical results for individual products are likely to be less accurate than those for the total.

CHAPTER 5

The Service Sector

It is commonly, and mistakenly, supposed that the service sector of the economy is not susceptible to productivity measurement because it does not produce quantifiable units of output.

The service sector is a conglomeration, a melange, a hodge-podge of activities. It would be more accurate to call it the "non-goods-producing" sector because it does in fact include all the industries except agriculture, mining, construction, and manufacturing, which make up the "goods producing" sector of the economy. The service sector includes trucking, railroads, communications, utilities, insurance, banking, trade, hotels, repair services, medical services, legal services, and many other activities.

To say that the sector is susceptible to measurement does not signify that the job will be easy. The difficulties of conceptualizing, defining, and measuring output and productivity vary widely among the industries. Because of the great diversity of activities this guidebook does not attempt to provide specific (and numerous) possible solutions but offers some guidelines for the service manager.

The guidelines are directed at three broad categories of service activities:

1. Identifiable physical units of service.

2. Intangible units of service.

3. The arts.

But first we shall discuss the deflation of dollar value of output, which is necessary in all categories.

Deflating Dollar Value of Service

Some significant work has been performed by economists on the subject of measuring productivity in service industries.[1] They have, for the most part, based their measures on constant-dollar value of output. This measure requires that a price index be available (or be constructed) to deflate the dollar-value receipts, transactions, or other measure.

The use of constant-dollar value of output as the basis for measuring productivity in a service industry or service establishment is certainly acceptable, as long as (1) the value of output does a reasonably adequate job of reflecting quality change and (2) the price index used for deflation captures the critically important elements of product mix and quality change. The necessary ingredients for this are often not available, especially for the statistician who must rely on a mass of data collected for a variety of purposes.

At the establishment level it is relatively feasible to identify and count the changes in variety of final services performed. The element of quality change, however, still poses very difficult problems for pricing. If the price of a visit to the doctor's office goes from $8.00 to $10.00 it is easy for the patient to comprehend that there has been a 25-percent increase in the cost of a visit to the doctor. If, however, we are concerned with the issue of productivity we need to know something about the quality of services performed in the doctor's office. In fact, if a particular ailment is now "cured" in one rather than the two visits previously required, the price per visit has increased from $8.00 to $10.00, but the "price" per cure has decreased from $16.00 to $10.00.

Physical Units of Service

Many establishments in the service sector produce a unit of service which is clearly identifiable and often quantifiable. Examples of industries in which such establishments are located and their units of output are the following: transportation, ton-miles of

---

[1] See for example, PRODUCTION AND PRODUCTIVITY IN THE SERVICE INDUSTRIES, Victor R. Fuchs, ed., 1969; and PRODUCTIVITY DIFFERENCES WITHIN THE SERVICE SECTOR, by Victor R. Fuchs and Jean Alexander Wilburn, 1967, both published by the National Bureau of Economic Research.

goods transported; utilities, cubic feet of gas or units of electric power; communication, telephone calls; barber shops, haircuts.

The ease, or difficulty, of measurement is not the same in each case. In the telephone industry a variety of services are performed—local and long-distance calls, direct dialing versus operator-assisted, weather and time reporting. Each of these has different input requirements, i.e., makes a different value (physical or dollar) contribution to output, and must be weighted accordingly. In this industry, the major technological changes which have occurred require that the weights be periodically examined and adjusted. The transition in long-distance calls from operator-assisted to direct dialing should be reflected as a productivity improvement. After a while, however, the weight for long-distance calls should be reduced because they no longer require as much input as they did when operators were required on every call.

In establishments such as barber shops it would not be too difficult to identify different units of output, such as flat tops, crew cuts, hair stylings, shampoos, and regular cuts. The major difficulty would be to keep a record of the different types of service. Even this could be relatively simple if the shop owner wanted a record of the shop's output and productivity. As each transaction was rung up on the cash register it could be coded for type of service and then tallied.

Once the units of service are identified, the procedures for measurement are exactly the same as for a plant which manufactures commodities.

Intangible Services

There are thousands of establishments in many different industries producing a service with a market value (it is purchased by the consumer), often with a recognizable physical form and yet extremely difficult to quantify and measure.

The reason frequently given for nonmeasurement of these activities is that there is no definable, quantifiable unit of output. The more likely reason is that there is often more than one way to identify or define output of an establishment and it is difficult to make a choice. Another important factor is that each unit of output is often subject to a wide band of quality, and the quality is difficult to evaluate and measure.

Medical and health services are an example of this difficult-to-measure category. Health service is the result of inputs from a variety of sources—doctors, hospitals, druggists, drug manufacturers. If all of them were to be included in the input part of the productivity ratio, what would the output be? In this case it might be logical to use the population death rate as an inverse measure of health care. But then we would have to consider the impact of pollution, public health services, diet, and other factors.

It is useful to make a distinction between the measurement objectives of the economist or sociologist and those of the administrator of a particular service. The former may be concerned with an output measure which reflects service to the community at large. The administrator can sharpen and pinpoint his attention to an examination of what his particular service unit is required to do.

The hospital administrator may be able to develop such measures of output as patient-days of hospital care. Different types of patient requirements would require different types of care. So the output measurement system would require different weights for different illnesses, operations, accidents, and other service requirements.

This measure is not foolproof. If surgical procedures change so that for some types of operations a patient is discharged two days earlier, the output per man-hour for that operation and post operative care may decline! The most intensive care is usually given in the first few days of hospitalization. The final days are periods of recovery requiring fewer hours of nursing and other care. If the hospital stay is reduced, the number of hours of patient care is reduced, but the average number per patient-day will rise.

Auto repair shops provide an illustration of many kinds of output that are subject to great variation in quality. Nevertheless, the industry has obviously developed some method of equating different types of repair jobs. Every auto repair shop has a standard guide book or manual on the cost of parts and labor for different repair operations on different makes and models of automobiles.

Shops may vary somewhat from the manual in their charges to the customer, but the labor components of the price of a tune-up, new water pump, carburetor, and similar work are often remarkably similar from one shop to the next. (The price of body repairs required after an accident is another story!)

The measurement task for the manager or administrator at his place of business is, in some ways, easier than that of the economist or statistician. In the latter case, the analyst may have little or no means of evaluating the quality of service or workmanship even if he can collect all of the quantitative data he might need. At the establishment, the manager can observe and make some judgment about the quality of work and may be able to install procedures for monitoring and measuring it.

Guidelines for Measuring Complex Services

There are no magic methods of measurement for complex service activities. There are no instant and easy formulas. The manager who wishes to examine the productivity progress of his institution may find a method which suits his particular needs. But if he wishes to compare his performance with that of other institutions, the methods of calculation among the different institutions must be compatible. Achieving compatability will require the cooperation of members of the industry, on their own initiative, or with the advice and guidance of a third party, or a combination of the two.

The data requirements for measuring changes in productivity may be somewhat easier to meet than the data requirements for measuring levels of productivity. However, the need for measures of productivity levels is very great, particularly among local government officials who are concerned with the rising costs of government services. The performance evaluation capability of city managements would be greatly enhanced if they could compare the productivity and cost of their city services with those of other cities—of trash removal, fire protection, police protection, education, and street and road maintenance. Each of these requires its own system of measurement, although the systems may have common procedural characteristics.

One system or method which may have the best chance of immediate applicability is the measurement of the performance of different components of a complex service activity. For example, in hospitals one might measure separately food distribution, laundry, trash removal, and other auxiliary services. This method admittedly tends to evade the basic question of overall final performance.

At the level of the enterprise the manager may be able to establish standards of performance, based on development of a theoretical standard or on performance in a time period which is selected as the standard base. This should be done in consultation with various levels of supervision as well as with workers. Productivity progress is measured at later periods by determining the deviation from standard.

This method may be as crude or as refined as the manager thinks he needs for management purposes. He is in a position to make judgmental adjustments if necessary. However, if the figures are to be used in any way as guides to wages or for comparison with the rest of the industry, the use of crudely contrived measures is severely limited.

For many types of services it will not be possible to develop a single, simple measure of output. However for many services it should be possible to develop a measure, perhaps complex in concept and computation, that will be comprehended by and useful to the service manager and his constituency. This measure will have two technical characteristics. (1) It will follow the principle of equivalents. (2) It will be derived through a scheme of multiple weighting.

The principle of equivalents has already been described in Chapter 3, but there is a variation which may be useful for some types of activities. Electric utilities, for example, deliver kilowatt-hours (KWH) of electricity. The input requirements per KWH vary with the size of the consumer. There is a higher input per KWH delivered to the single-family residence than to the average commercial and industrial establishment. Services provided to rural electrification customers are broken down even further into large and small commercial and industrial units and consumers engaged in irrigation activities.

The equivalents for these different services were established by the Bureau of Labor Statistics in consultation with the industry. The output measure is the sum of the weighted units of service; that is, for each class of service (or customer) the number of KWH is multiplied by an appropriate equivalent weight.

The principle of multiple weighting might be regarded as another variation of the principle of equivalents, but whatever the name it is a useful technique. It is now followed in the measurement of output in transportation. The measure used, ton-miles, combines the elements of distance and weight of merchandise transported.

This may ultimately be the only way of arriving at an output measure that will reasonably satisfy the advocates of different units of measurement. It is unlikely that a unit of final output can be adequately isolated, identified, and measured in many of the complex service activities. Rather, the components of output or the different qualities of an output can be identified and assigned appropriate (although approximate) weights. The result is not a ton or mile of freight but a ton-mile of freight. In the hospital each illness, operation, and accident will have assigned to it standard, weighted factors decided on by experts in statistics, medical care, and administration.

The following list is illustrative of the kinds of factors that might be considered for multiple weighting among different types of activities. It is only illustrative; in some cases other factors not shown may be as important as, or more so than, the ones listed.

Trade	Number of sales; self-service v. use of salespersons; value of sale; type of merchandise.
Banking	Number of accounts; number of checks handled; value of accounts and checks (if a factor); savings v. checking accounts; loans; size of loans.
Insurance	Policies active; value of policies; type of insurance (life, accident, property); claims paid; value of claims.
Hotels	Size of hotel; quality class; number of rooms rented; availability of meal service; occupancy per room; complaints (to be subtracted).

Laundries	Type of laundry (e.g., shirts v. flats); volume; collection and delivery v. customer-performed; complaints (subtraction).
Secondary schools	Size of student body; number of graduates; characteristics of the community; grades on Standard Achievement Test.
Trash removal and disposal	Volume collected; frequency of collection; cleanliness of streets; curbstone v. backyard collection; population density and other community characteristics.

This list of items does not specifically take account of increasing or decreasing quality of service. To a certain extent shoddy service will have an impact on labor input (and thus reduce the productivity rate) because of the time required to rectify bad performance. Complaints about service might also be used as a subtraction from output or kept as a separate tally for final judgmental evaluations.

The Arts

There is a segment of the service sector which is not covered by any of the previous discussion. That segment includes the activities known as the arts—painting, ballet, orchestras, and the like.

It is hoped that the managers of these types of enterprises will continue to give most of their attention to the recruitment, development, and "management" of the talent required to please the eye and ear of the beholder; that they will continue to give some of their attention to the administrative costs of the enterprise so that the entertainment they offer can be available to a large part of the population.

It is also hoped that managers will give little of their time and attention to the productivity of their performers as productivity is customarily conceived and defined. We do not wish to have the Minute Waltz performed in 46 seconds.

CHAPTER 6

Other Inputs

Management is often interested in examining its firm's performance by relating output to resources or inputs other than a straight count of man-hours. The interest is likely to be in inputs such as quality or value of labor, capital, materials or some combination of them. Measures of these inputs in the firm or industry differ in concept from man-hour figures. The former are constant-dollar value of inputs; the latter are "physical" units of input.

The cost of labor at any given period is the price (wages and salaries and other monetary benefits) paid to labor in that period. Employment costs per unit are expressed as a ratio of total dollars spent on payrolls and supplements to the volume of output. Similarly for materials. Similarly for capital, although here the measurement of costs is much more complex because capital equipment (or structures or land) is purchased at one time but used for a long period.

When measures of productivity are computed by using labor value, capital, materials, or a combination of these, the value of the inputs is expressed in constant dollars. Therefore, they are not measures of current costs per unit of output. This distinction should be kept in mind not only when measuring but also when analyzing the significance of the various productivity trends using inputs other than a straight count of man-hours.

Weighted Man-hours

The common measure of output per man-hour uses the man-hours of all employees without differentiation as to their quality.

46

One man-hour of unskilled labor has the same value as one man-hour of a skilled machinist, or of a secretary or plant manager.

Quite often the occupational mix of the firm changes for reasons which may be related to productivity. Higher output per man-hour may be achieved by new technology which requires greater skill from the work force. (Sometimes, it is claimed, a lower degree of skill is required.) Job simplification or job enrichment might change the occupational structure. In these cases it may be desirable to construct a measure of productivity which takes account of the change in skill requirements and occupational structure.

There are various ways of obtaining a measure which reflects the change in the quality of employment. One which might be most meaningful for the firm is to utilize its occupational classification system. Each occupational class is assigned a weight, usually the wage rate for the base period.[1] In computing changes, the man-hours in the base period in each occupational class are multiplied by the weight for that class, and the weighted figures are summed. The man-hours for the next and subsequent periods are multiplied by those same weights, and so on (Table 9). The technique is essentially the same as that used to derive weighted output.

Since the measure uses a base-year wage rate, it is affected only by changes in the occupational structure and not by general wage changes. If the firm maintains a wage-rate index, it can use that index to deflate current payrolls (or compensation) and so avoid the task of weighting man-hours by base-year occupational wage rates. However, it must be a wage (or compensation) *rate* index, not an average hourly earnings index. The latter is affected by both wage rate and occupational changes and if used for deflation would yield a measure of straight man-hours.

The data in Table 9 indicate a very wide occupational wage differential and a relatively sharp shift in occupational structure. In the more typical case there is, of course, a much larger list of occupational classes with a smaller wage spread between classes, at least at the lower levels. Consequently, it is likely that the difference

---

[1] A more comprehensive and "better" weight would be compensation per man-hour, to reflect difference in fringes as well as basic hourly rates. This method also implicitly assumes that hourly rates are a reflection of occupational productivity (i.e., quality) differences.

between a weighted and unweighted labor productivity measure would be less than that shown.

Table 9.   Calculation of Weighted Man-Hours

| | | Period 1 | | Period 2 | |
| | | Number of Man-Hours | | Number of Man-Hours | |
Occupation	Wage Rate	Actual	Weighted	Actual	Weighted
(1)	(2)	(3)	(2)×(3) (4)	(5)	(2)×(5) (6)
Laborer	$2.00	13	26	10	20
Machine operator	4.00	8	32	10	40
Machinist	6.00	2	12	4	24
Totals		23	70	24	84

From Table 9 we calculate:

Index of man-hours $= (24 \div 23)\ 100 = 104.3$
Index of weighted man-hours $= (84 \div 70)\ 100 = 120.0$

If output in that firm had increased by 26 percent, we would have:

Index of output $= 126.0$
Index of output per man-hour $= (126.0 \div 104.3)\ 100 = 120.8$
Index of output per weighted
man-hour $= (126.0 \div 120.0)\ 100 = 105.0$

Another method that has been used to measure change in the quality of labor is the classification of workers by age, sex, and education in each period and the assignment of a base-year value to each category for use as weights.[2] This type of measure is more useful to economists than to managers and is not recommended for the latter.

In any case, the plant manager or other official or analyst in the firm should decide for himself the usefulness of a "weighted" man-hour measure, recognizing that he can more easily prepare two other measures, output per dollar of payroll and output per man-hour. These two figures span the gap from a measure of employment costs to an indicator of physical resource requirements.

---

[2] Edward Denison, THE SOURCES OF ECONOMIC GROWTH IN THE UNITED STATES AND THE ALTERNATIVES BEFORE US (New York, 1962).

Materials

It is quite common to relate cost of materials to value of output, both in current dollars. This ratio can be affected by change in price or in physical volume of either output or materials input. If the manager wishes to examine the materials-output relationship more intensively, it may be useful to break the ratio down into its price and volume components.

A first step is the derivation of an output measure in constant, physical terms. This will already have been done if output per man-hour measures have been computed. The ratio now computable is current cost of materials per unit of output, which can be useful for cost analysis.

Current value (cost) of materials may be split into "price" and physical unit components in exactly the same way as was done for output. In this case we either deflate or use a weighted measure. The objective is to calculate physical or constant-dollar measure of output per unit of materials.

For deflation it is necessary that the firm have, or develop, a price index for cost of materials. For a weighted measure, number of units of materials purchased, by type or class, and a unit value for each type or class are required.

Whether deflation or unit weights are used, it is important that the two measures, materials and output in constant prices, be compatible. Otherwise, distortions can arise in the resultant ratios of output per dollar (constant) of materials. This issue can be a bit tricky because it becomes involved with alternative index-number concepts and procedures. The alternative index numbers are referred to as "base-year weighted" and "current-year weighted."

In some establishments different raw or semiprocessed materials are used for the different final outputs, and there may be significant differences in the relationship between material costs and final value of output. The price trends among the various materials purchased may also differ.

In Chapter 3 illustrations were given of the development of output measures in base-year values by the method of weighting, that is, by multiplying units of output by base-year unit values. In Table 10 it is shown how output and input measures in base-year prices are obtained by deflation in two steps:

1) A price index with *current*-year weights is constructed.

2) This price index is used to deflate current-year values, i.e., to convert them to base-year prices; current-year value is divided by the price index to obtain indexes of materials and output in base-year prices.

Table 10.   Calculating Price Indexes and Deflated Value for Materials Input and Output

I. Detailed Data

Item	Year 1			Year 5			
			Value				Value
	Price	Pounds	Year 1 Weights	Year 5 Weights	Price	Pounds	Year 5 Weights
	(1)	(2)	$(1) \times (2)$ (3)	$(1) \times (6)$ (4)	(5)	(6)	$(5) \times (6)$ (7)
Materials input							
Cattle	.20	250	$50	$60	.25	300	$75
Hogs	.15	100	15	18	.20	120	24
Total			$65	$78			$99
Output							
Beef	.40	150	$60	$80	.42	200	$84
Pork	.30	80	24	30	.35	100	35
Total			$84	$110			$119

II. Index Calculations

Item	Dollars		Index
	Year 1	Year 5	Year 5
	(8)	(9)	(10)
In current dollars			
Materials	65	99	152.3
Output	84	119	141.7
Materials per unit of output	.774	.832	107.5
Current-year quantity weighted prices			
Materials	78	99	126.9
Output	110	119	108.2
Deflated values—Year 1 and 5 in base-year prices			
Materials	65	78	120.0
Output	84	110	131.0
Materials per unit of output	.774	.709	91.6

It may be noted that price indexes with base-year quantity weights can be used to deflate (inflate) base-year value of materials and output to obtain base-year data in current-year prices. Most government price indexes for groups of commodities or for industries are of the base-year-weighted type. It may also be noted that the technique for constructing a price index is the same as that for constructing a productivity index, and much of the same data are required.

Capital Input

Examination of capital productivity also begins with the more familiar concept of an operating ratio—capital costs as a percentage of value of sales (or of production). In this ratio each year's output is measured in the actual dollars of that year (i.e., current-year dollars). The value of capital is measured in accordance with the company's accounting practices—usually in terms of replacement costs.

The development of a capital productivity ratio proceeds in several stages from the operating ratio. The concepts, and measurement, of capital are among the most complex of the various inputs and outputs that might be encountered in systems of productivity measurement. Therefore, before discussing methodology it may be useful to discuss some concepts.

There are various types of assets which appear in a firm's balance sheet and which represent investment capital. We shall consider these in the section on total-factor productivity below, but for the time being we shall consider only fixed capital assets—land, plant, and machinery and equipment.

The most inflexible of fixed capital assets, in terms of ease of replacement, is land; next is plant. Equipment is usually (although not always) replaceable within the given land and plant structure. Consequently, in measuring month-to-month or year-to-year changes in capital and capital productivity, the firm may wish to consider some set of measures which deal only with equipment.

The value of capital equipment usually is expressed in terms of the value of capital stock on hand. But there are two alternatives possible within this stock concept, gross and net. Gross value of stock retains the full value of each piece of equipment for its lifetime. The value is removed from the books when the equipment is removed physically from the premises. Net value of stock retains only the depreciated value of the stock on the books, which means that fully depreciated capital equipment may remain in use but have no value in the capital accounts.

Another concept of capital is the flow, rather than the stock, of capital. In this case the annual (or monthly) depreciation value would be used. Value of capital stock or depreciation includes value of equipment which remains idle while no production is taking place, even during a plant shutdown. Another concept of capital, which is considered by some to be more closely related to the productivity concept, is a measure which reflects the value of capital only as it is used in the production process. However, this seems a very impractical kind of measure. The equipment remains within the establishment; it is not mobile, cannot move to other locations, and because of obsolescence factors continues to depreciate in value even though it is not utilized.

A measure of physical capital which is equivalent in concept to a man-hour weighted measure of output embraces the concept of "embodied labor"; that is, the man-hours required in the manufacture of the equipment are used as the measure of capital input. This is also an impractical measure; it is too difficult to obtain and is not particularly useful for the individual firm.

It appears that some measure of capital stock may be the most appropriate for measuring capital productivity. Each of the two choices available, gross and net, presents its own problems. Gross value of stock may overstate true value if the equipment has deteriorated and is operating inefficiently. Net stock value can be affected by company accounting practices and by changes in those practices, especially when depreciation tax laws are revised, and may understate true value, as indicated earlier. There is no special solution available for this problem. The decision as to which measure to use depends on the firm's accounting practices and the judgment of its personnel.

So we come then to a measure of the stock of capital in constant prices. The objective is to value all capital equipment at a base-year price. The method of doing this depends on the firm's accounting practices. Alternatively, a new set of accounts can be established for this purpose.

If the accounting procedures are such that all equipment is regularly revalued at current replacement costs, this is equivalent to capital equipment stock in current-year prices (current dollars). A price index is needed to reduce (deflate) the current value to base-year prices. This is likely to be a difficult, complicated procedure.

The easiest method to follow would be to use an equipment price index already constructed by someone else. The most comprehensive and reliable source of indexes of this type is the Bureau of Labor Statistics' Wholesale Price Index and its components, in particular its machinery component. However, these government-compiled indexes are intended to reflect average price movements in the United States as a whole, and it would be fortuitous if they were applicable to the stock of equipment of any single firm. The smaller the firm and the more specialized its equipment, the less likely it is that a general price index will be applicable.

It is possible that the price trend for specific machinery commodities as published by the U. S. Government can be used to deflate the specific units or groups of units within a firm. In this case compatibility and adequacy of coverage would have to be established. For most companies this is also not likely to be a fruitful source of capital-equipment deflators.

An alternative is to develop a price index specifically for the equipment owned by the establishment. The firm can maintain its own price data or obtain it from equipment manufacturers for each piece of equipment. It would then have to construct an index to reflect the mix of the stock of equipment whose total value is to be deflated. The method is basically the same as that shown earlier for calculating a price index for materials input or for output.

If stocks of capital are retained on the accounting books in terms of their original purchase price, each unit of equipment must be revalued to a base-year price. This can be done by obtaining a price index for each type and deflating; or by obtaining a base-year price by estimation or from the equipment manufacturer.

The last possibility in effect amounts to setting up an additional set of accounts for capital equipment. As each new piece of equipment is added to the firm's stock, a base-year price for it is determined and it is placed in the base-year-priced set of capital accounts.

There is an interesting conceptual and procedural nuance here which should not be overlooked. Quite often new equipment is not merely a replica of the existing stock of equipment. It is usually a newer, more efficient model which supplements or replaces the old equipment. The greater efficiency is usually represented by greater capacity within any given unit of time. That greater capacity should not be translated into higher dollar value unless more resources (labor, materials, etc.) were used in the manufacture of the new equipment. The improved efficiency is the same as improved productivity. If the value of that improvement were always added, output per unit of capital would remain stable by definition and the method would be self-defeating.

The purpose of this procedure is to measure changes in capital stock in constant prices. The alternatives described have been directed at converting stocks to base-year prices; that is, the physical stocks of capital in the current year and in the base year are expressed in base-year prices. This means that the value of stock (in base-year prices) is always comparable from one year to the next.

There is another alternative which would measure the capital stock in current-year prices. In this case the value of capital equipment in the base year is converted each year. The base year is "inflated," assuming that prices have risen, to the current year's prices. In this method, the base year is comparable with each current year, but the year-to-year measures of stock are not strictly comparable because they are expressed in differing-year prices.

The method chosen for pricing capital input should be consistent with the method chosen for pricing output. Both should be in base-year prices or both in current-year prices. With these data, output per dollar of capital—the capital productivity ratio—can be computed.

These procedures may appear to be cumbersome and time-consuming—and they are. They might be costly to put into effect and to maintain. The manager has to decide whether the information is worth the cost of record keeping and computation or whether the ratio he started with—capital costs as a percentage of value of output—is adequate for management and cost control purposes.

Total-Factor Productivity

Much interest has developed in recent years in a concept of productivity known as total-factor productivity. The measurement, in principle, would relate output to all inputs but in practice it may relate output to labor plus selected components of capital. The concept has been of particular interest to economists concerned with evaluating the change in efficiency of production of the economy, since it reflects the costs (in constant dollars) of all the input factors—capital, labor and other inputs. There has also been interest in this measure as it might relate to the issue of productivity and wages.

This author has some reservations about the usefulness of a total-factor productivity measure at the level of the firm. Attention is once more called to the difference between costs and productivity. The cost of labor plus capital, or labor plus materials, or labor plus capital plus materials *in current dollars* per unit of output are all ratios of unit costs. A productivity ratio which combines any two or three of these is in essence a ratio of the physical quantities of input per unit of physical output or, more accurately, value of input in constant dollars per unit of output; or the inverse, output per unit of all factors of input stated in constant prices. Some companies construct and use indexes of total-factor productivity, but it may be difficult to utilize this ratio for management- or financial-control purposes without first breaking it down into each of its components, output per unit of labor, of capital, and of materials.

In examining the efficiency and costs of his operation, the manager may quite properly be interested in the extent to which one factor is being substituted for another. The relative costs of labor, capital, and materials are of great importance. He may also find it useful to analyze the changing costs of the inputs combined and separately in terms of both their prices and quantities.

A measure of total-factor productivity which relates output to labor plus capital requires that the output and input be expressed in constant dollars and, obviously, that labor and capital be combined in constant-dollar terms. The essential ingredients of data on labor and fixed capital equipment required for this ratio under several systems of accounting have already been discussed in this chapter. Procedures have been described for expressing quantity or value of labor in base-year wages and value of capital equipment in base-year prices. If these procedures are followed, labor and capital equipment will each be expressed in compatible value terms, and they could simply be added together to obtain a measure of labor plus capital input. This simple addition would, however, give an undue amount of weight to capital equipment (which has been measured as stock of capital). More sophisticated procedures are required.

Value of labor in constant prices has been determined by multiplying current man-hours times base-year earnings per man-hour. The earnings rate is, in effect, a base-year rate of return to labor; the aggregate earnings represent a portion of output in constant dollars. We wish to add a similar type of figure for value of capital.

We must first calculate a base-year rate of return to capital based on the ratio of income before taxes to capital investment. That rate is applied each year to the value of capital in constant, base-year prices in order to obtain what is equivalent to a capital-investment component which is to be added to the weighted labor component.

Keep in mind that the capital and income figures should be related to production, not to sales, in the base period. Therefore, any margin accruing to the firm in the base period because of use of inventory should be subtracted from income (or added if the margin was negative). Also, income is affected by book value of depreciation. If the base-year value of depreciation is higher than the book value, the difference should be subtracted from income.

This procedure might also "over-weight" capital equipment investment relative to labor input; the degree will depend on the ratio of machinery and equipment to total capital investment, labor, and materials. In order to obtain a better perspective on this matter, it is useful to proceed first to a discussion of total-factor productivity in which all inputs are counted. We will then return to the more limited measure.

Table 11.   Total-Factor Productivity

I. Balance Sheet, Income and Rates of Return

Item	Base Year (1)	Year T [1] (2)
A. Balance sheet items—assets		
1. Cash and marketable securities	$ 22,000	$ 28,000
2. Accounts receivable	65,000	80,000
3. Inventories—materials and supplies	25,000	30,000
4. Inventories—finished goods and goods in process	70,000	85,000
5. All other assets except fixed	18,000	17,000
Subtotal	200,000	240,000
6. Fixed: a) land, plant and equipment	150,000	160,000
b) machinery and equipment only	80,000	90,000
7. Total assets	350,000	400,000
B. Capital investment income		
8. Income before taxes	$ 50,000	
9. Less: margin on inventory	1,860	
10. Less: base year minus book value of depreciation	40	
11. Adjusted capital investment	48,100	54,800 [2]
C. Rate of return on capital investment (percent)		
12. On total assets (11 ÷ 7)	13.7	
13. On fixed assets		
a) total fixed (11 ÷ 6a)	32.1	
b) machinery and equipment (11 ÷ 6b)	60.0	

[1] In base-year prices.

[2] Computed: Base-year rate of return on total assets times Year T assets in base-year prices (Line 12 times Line 7, Col. 2).

Table 11—Contd.

II. Outputs, Inputs, and Productivity Ratios

D. Output

14. Output (sales adjusted for inventory)	$400,000	$480,000

E. Inputs

15. Materials and supplies	149,900	164,000
16. Purchased services	40,000	42,000
17. Depreciation	8,000	8,600
18. Interest and sundry	6,000	6,600
19. Labor (all wages and salaries)	148,000	156,000
20. Capital investment income [3]	48,100	54,800 [4]
21. Total all inputs	400,000	432,000

F. Capital investment income

22. Total assets @ 13.7 percent	$ 48,100	54,800 [4]
23. Fixed assets @ 32.1 percent	48,100	51,360 [4]
24. Machinery and equipment @ 60.0 percent	48,100	54,000 [4]

G. Combined capital investment income plus labor

25. Total assets (line 19 plus 22)	196,100	210,800
26. Fixed assets (line 19 plus 23)	196,100	207,360
27. Machinery and equipment (line 19 plus 24)	196,100	210,000

H. Productivity ratios—output (line 14) related to:

28. All inputs (Line 21)	1.00	1.11
29. Labor plus		
a) total capital investment income (line 25)	2.04	2.28
b) fixed assets (line 26)	2.04	2.31
c) machinery and equipment (line 27)	2.04	2.29
30. Labor only (line 19)	2.70	3.08

[3] Same as Line B11 and F22.
[4] Computed. Base-year rate of return (Section C) times Lines A7, 6a and 6b.

Table 11 presents a series of balance-sheet and income statistics most of which are based on the annual report of a diversified corporation, with estimates for some of the detailed components. All data are shown in base-year prices. Methods of converting data to base-year prices have already been described for labor, materials, and machinery and equipment. For the other items listed the following types of deflators might be used:

Cash and securities and accounts receivable—GNP (private) deflator.

Inventories; materials and supplies—materials price index previously computed.

Inventories; finished goods—output price index previously computed.

Inventories; goods in process—average of materials and output price indexes.

Plant—construction cost index (e.g., from *Engineering News Record*). Note that most publicly available construction cost indexes have serious deficiencies.

Land—Index of current value divided by base-year value. (Deflated rental value may be used in lieu of deflated value of land.)

Purchased services—depends on type of services purchased. Materials or output price indexes or a wage index, or some combination might be most appropriate.

Interest—GNP (private) deflator, or an interest-rate index.

Total assets in the base year were equal to $350,000 (A.7). The company's profit and loss statement showed a profit (i.e., net income) before taxes of $50,000 in the base year (B.8). After the price adjustment for inventory and depreciation, the adjusted income was $48,100 (B.11). This will be the base-year "capital investment income."

We can now calculate a rate of return on total investment— 13.7 percent (C.12). We can also calculate rates of return on fixed capital or on machinery and equipment only (C.13) by using the same adjusted income figure.

When capital investment is added to all the other inputs (E.15-20), the total of inputs (E.21) is in balance with the value of output (D.14), all in base-year prices.

To compute total-factor productivity in Year T we consider or calculate the following (all in base-year prices).

1. Output in Year T is equal to $480,000 (D.14).
2. All inputs, other than income, are obtained from the accounts and converted to base-year prices (E.15-19).
3. The value of assets in constant dollars has increased from $350,000 to $400,000 (A.7).

4. The rate of return applied to total assets yields an adjusted income of $54,800 (B.11 and E.20). This is the income (adjusted, in base-year prices) that would have been received in the base year, at base-year efficiency in utilization of inputs, but with Year T mix of assets.

5. The total of inputs, including capital investment in Year T, is $432,000 (E.21).

6. The total-factor productivity ratio of 1.11 (H.28) for Year T is value of output divided by value of inputs as computed.

7. The index of total-factor productivity for Year T is 111.0 (H.28 Col. 2 divided by Col. 1, times 100).

It was indicated earlier that rates of return can be calculated on something less than total assets, specifically on fixed assets or on machinery and equipment only, in the base year. These rates of return, when applied to Year T asset figures (in base-year prices), yield investment-income figures which are slightly different from total investment income. That is because the different types of assets increased at different rates between the base year and Year T.

So-called "partial productivity" ratios (H.29, 30), indexes, and percent changes can now also be calculated and compared by relating output to different inputs. Labor productivity rose 14.1 percent; labor-plus-machinery-and-equipment productivity rose 12.3 percent; total-factor productivity rose 11.1 percent (Col.2 divided by Col.1).

CHAPTER 7

Government Productivity Statistics

The official source of U.S. Government statistics on productivity is the Bureau of Labor Statistics (BLS) of the U.S. Department of Labor. That agency publishes indexes of output per man-hour at varying time intervals for different parts of the economy. There are two major types of indexes published or made available by the BLS—indexes for the economy and major industry sectors and indexes for individual industries.[1]

Economy-Wide and Sector Indexes

The BLS publishes indexes of output per man-hour for the total private economy and for the nonfarm and manufacturing and corporate sectors each quarter. It also publishes annual indexes for additional sectors at irregular intervals, depending on the availability of data from the U.S. Department of Commerce. These other sectors are mining, transportation and utilities, and trade. Indexes for other sectors, construction, finance, insurance and real estate, services, and government, are not published because of data deficiencies.

The description which follows relates to the economy and sector measures, except as noted at the end of the section.

Output per man-hour, for these measures, refers to the constant-dollar value of goods and services produced per man-hour. The latter includes the hours of all persons employed (including proprietors and unpaid family workers).

The output component of these productivity indexes is computed from U.S. Department of Commerce figures on gross national

___
[1] See list of references at end of this chapter.

product for the total private economy and for each of the sectors, technically referred to as "gross national product originating in the sector." It comprises the final purchase of goods and services by consumers, gross private domestic investment (including the change in business inventories), net foreign investment, and government, all deflated separately for changes in prices.

Final goods and services are differentiated from intermediate products in that they are usually not purchased for further fabrication or resale. In addition to purchases in the market, final goods and services include some items provided but not actually purchased, such as food furnished to employees, food produced and consumed on farms, and the rental value of owner-occupied homes.

Measures for the individual sectors are derived by subtracting the constant-dollar value of goods and services purchased by the sector from the constant-total-dollar value of products and services produced by the sector, where such a method is feasible. Because of data limitations, actual measures are derived by means of other approaches which attempt to approximate this concept.

In the service sector, where measures of physical units of output or service have not been adequately developed, it is customary to use some price indexes which may be conceptually inadequate for deflation or to use employment trends as an indicator of service output trends.

In the construction industry value of output is deflated by a price index which is really a cost index. This index is for the most part based on costs of labor and materials combined in terms of some base-period weighting. It does not take account of savings in materials or labor, and as a result the price increase is overstated. Consequently, output and productivity gains are understated.

For government, the practice in the national income accounts is to value government output in terms of wages or salaries of government employees. Since these are expressed in constant dollars, they turn out to be equivalent to the trend in employment. This obviously leads to a ratio, output per unit of employment, for which the possibilities of increase (or decrease) have been ruled out by statistical definition.[1]

---

[1] Except to the extent that there is an upward occupational shift which is not removed in the "deflation" process.

The BLS does not publish productivity indexes for these sectors because it considers the output measures inadequate for that purpose.

The labor input measures for the published series are based largely on a monthly survey of establishment payroll records. Since this survey does not cover total employment in the private economy and because there are gaps in the hours information, some supplementary data are used to derive man-hours estimates for all persons engaged in producing the output of the private economy. Various sources are utilized, and data from them are adjusted for consistency with the establishment man-hours.

The establishment man-hours are based on an hours-paid rather than an hours-worked concept. That is, the estimates include paid holidays, vacations, sick leave, and other time off paid for by the employer in addition to actual hours worked.

Industry Productivity Indexes

The BLS publishes annual indexes of output per man-hour for a group of industries based on the "physical units of output" of those industries. These measures are closest in concept and methodology to the establishment indexes described in this booklet.

For most of the industries the output component of the productivity ratio is derived by combining different commodities, products, or units of service (e.g., in transportation) with unit value or unit man-hour weights. The BLS attempts, in these measures, to use methods which eliminate the effects of shifts among products with different values per man-hour. It is not always completely successful because detailed product and/or weighting information is sometimes not available.

In fact, the list of published industry indexes is as small as it is (about 35 industries) because of the inadequacies of available data. Except in a few special cases the BLS does not collect its own production statistics but relies on data available from other government agencies, principally the Bureau of the Census. Quite often the data available do not provide sufficient detail for quality change, unit-value of man-hour weights, shifts of products within product classes, and other technical matters.

The BLS has, for several years, maintained a set of productivity indexes for over 300 manufacturing industries for analytical purposes. These indexes are based on deflated value of shipments, and the resultant measures of constant-dollar output per man-hour are heavily dependent on the adequacy of the price indexes used for deflation. Sometimes the industry price indexes are based on coverage of only a small proportion of the industry's output. Again, important shifts among products of the industry may not be accounted for by the price index.

For these and other statistical reasons the BLS has not published this set of output-per-man-hour indexes. However, they have been considered generally reliable enough for cross-industry analysis, and the BLS has used them for such purposes (for example, in determining the relationship between changes in productivity and changes in employment).

In setting guidelines and developing procedures for determining allowable price increases under the Economic Stabilization Program, the Price Commission requested and obtained from the BLS (early in 1972) the indexes of output per man-hour for these 300-plus industries. Most of the index series covered the period 1958-1969. The indexes were utilized by staff members of the Price Commission to calculate average annual rates of change in productivity for each of the industries. These are the figures that are used by the Price Commission (at this writing) in reviewing applications from companies for price increases.

APPENDIX I

References

Productivity Publications of the
U.S. Department of Labor, Bureau of Labor Statistics

I. *General: Concepts and Techniques*

A. MEANING AND MEASUREMENT OF PRODUCTIVITY, BLS Bulletin 1714, a report prepared for the National Commission on Productivity by the Bureau of Labor Statistics, 1971. 30 cents.

B. "Output Per Man-Hour Measures: Private Sector," reprint of Chapter 25 of the HANDBOOK OF METHODS FOR SURVEYS AND STUDIES, BLS Bulletin 1711, 1971. Describes the methods used to derive productivity measures.

C. "Technical Note: Industry Indexes of Output Per Man-Hour," by Jerome A. Mark, *Monthly Labor Review,* November 1962, pp. 1269-73. Reprint 2404.

D. PRODUCTIVITY AND THE ECONOMY, BLS Bulletin 1710, 1971. 50 cents. A chartbook investigating productivity trends and their relation to other economic trends.

E. "Wage-Price Guidepost Statistics: Problems of Measurement," by Jerome A. Mark, before the American Statistical Association, Pittsburgh, Pa., August 1968.

F. "Sector Change in Unit Labor Costs," by Leon Greenberg and Jerome A. Mark, a reprint from THE INDUSTRIAL COMPOSITION OF INCOME AND PRODUCT (New York: National Bureau of Economic Research, 1968).

G. BLS Publications on Productivity and Technology 1972 (a listing of available publications).

II. *Productivity Indexes: The Economy and Major Sectors*

A. Indexes of Output Per Man-Hour, Hourly Compensation, and Unit Labor Costs in the Private Economy and the Nonfarm Sector. 1947 to the present. Quarterly and annual.

B. Indexes of Output Per Man-Hour, Hourly Compensation, and Unit Labor Costs in the Manufacturing Sectors. 1947 to the present. Quarterly and annual.

C. Productivity Trends in the U. S. 1909-70, Private Economy and Major Sectors (in process).

III. *Productivity Indexes: Individual Industries*

Indexes of Output Per Man-Hour for Selected Industries, 1939 and 1947-70, BLS Bulletin 1692, 1971. $1.25. Includes the following industries:

SIC Code	Industry	Reports Available
	Mining	
101	Iron mining, crude ore	
101	Iron mining, useable ore	
102	Copper mining, crude ore	
102	Copper mining, recoverable metal	
11, 12	Coal mining	
12	Bituminous coal and lignite mining	
	Manufacturing	
203	Canning and preserving	
2041	Flour and other grain mill products	
206	Sugar	*
2071	Candy and other confectionery products	
2082	Malt liquors	
2086	Bottled and canned soft drinks	*

SIC Code	Industry	Reports Available
211, 212, 213	Tobacco products: total	
211, 213	Cigarettes, chewing and smoking tobacco	
212	Cigars	
2251, 2252	Hosiery	*
261, 262, 263, 266	Paper, paperboard, and pulpmills	
2653	Corrugated and solid fiber boxes	*
2823, 2824	Man-made fibers	*
2911	Petroleum refining	
301	Tires and inner tubes	
314	Footwear	*
3221	Glass containers	
324	Cement, hydraulic	
3271, 3272	Concrete products	*
331	Steel	*
3321	Gray iron foundries	*
3331, 3332, 3333	Primary copper, lead, and zinc	
3334	Primary aluminum	*
3352	Aluminum rolling and drawing	*
3631, 3632, 3633, 3639	Major household appliances	*
3651	Radio and television receiving sets	*
371	Motor vehicles and equipment	*

Other

401	Railroad transportation, revenue traffic	
401	Railroad transportation, car-miles	*
451	Air transportation	*
4612, 4613	Petroleum pipelines	*
491, 492, 493	Gas and electric utilities	*

In Process

	Bakery products	*
	Metal cans	*

Ready-mix concrete   *
Intercity motor carriers   *
Nonmetallic minerals   *
Paints and varnishes   *
Steel foundries   *

---

* Separate reports on these industries are or will be available.

IV. *How To Order BLS Publications*

Priced publications are for sale by the Superintendent of Documents, U.S. Government Printing Office, Washington, D.C. 20402, or by any of the Bureau of Labor Statistics regional offices. Free publications are available as long as the supply lasts from either the Bureau of Labor Statistics, Washington, D.C. 20212, or from any of the Bureau's regional offices.

Selected Nongovernment References

THE SOURCES OF ECONOMIC GROWTH IN THE UNITED STATES AND THE ALTERNATIVES BEFORE US, by Edward F. Denison (Committee for Economic Development, 1962).

A PRIMER ON PRODUCTIVITY, by Solomon Fabricant (New York: Random House, 1969).

MEASURING COMPANY PRODUCTIVITY, by John W. Kendrick and Daniel Creamer (New York: National Industrial Conference Board, 1965).

PRODUCTION AND PRODUCTIVITY IN THE SERVICE INDUSTRIES, by Victor R. Fuchs (New York: National Bureau of Economic Research, 1969).

Algebra for Calculating Weighted Output per Man-Hour

Let: L = Unit man-hours for each product

Q = Number of units of product

Subscript o = Base period

Subscript i = Any other period

(1) $\dfrac{\Sigma\, L_oQ_i}{\Sigma\, L_oQ_o}$ = Index of output with base year unit man-hour weights

(2) $\dfrac{\Sigma\, L_iQ_i}{\Sigma\, L_oQ_o}$ = Index of man-hours

(3) $\dfrac{\Sigma\, L_iQ_i}{\Sigma\, L_oQ_o} \div \dfrac{\Sigma\, L_oQ_i}{\Sigma\, L_oQ_o} = \dfrac{\Sigma\, L_iQ_i}{\Sigma\, L_oQ_i}$ = Index of man-hours per unit of output (output in current-year quantities)

(Man-hours in current period compared with man-hours it would have taken in base period to produce the *current-year* market basket of goods.)

The inverse of man-hours per unit of output is:

(4) $\dfrac{\Sigma\, L_oQ_i}{\Sigma\, L_iQ_i}$ = Output per man-hour

(5) $\dfrac{\Sigma\, L_iQ_i}{\Sigma\, L_iQ_o}$ = Index of output with current-year weights

69

(6) $\dfrac{\Sigma\ L_iQ_i}{\Sigma\ L_oQ_o} \div \dfrac{\Sigma\ L_iQ_i}{\Sigma\ L_iQ_o} = \dfrac{\Sigma\ L_iQ_o}{\Sigma\ L_oQ_o} =$ Index of man-hours per unit of output (output in base-year quantities)

(Man-hours it would have taken in current period compared with man-hours it took in base period to produce *base-year* market basket of goods.)

And the inverse is:

(7) $\dfrac{\Sigma\ L_oQ_o}{\Sigma\ L_iQ_o} =$ Output per man-hour

Transforming Index Number to New Base Reference Year

The index for the base year (I_0) is always 100.

The index for any other year ($I_1, I_2, I_3 \ldots I_i$) is always an arithmetic relative of 100.

We wish to set $I_i = 100$.

All other indexes in the series must now be related to the new base.

$100 \div I_i = $ Factor.

New indexes = Factor times ($I_1, I_3, I_4 \ldots I_i$)

Example: *Old indexes*

> 1958 = 100 Old base
> 1963 — 115
> 1965 = 125 New base
> 1970 = 130
>
> $100 \div 125 = .80 = $ Factor

New indexes

> 1958 = 100 × .80 = 80
> 1963 = 115 × .80 = 92
> 1965 = 125 × .80 = 100
> 1970 = 130 × .80 = 104